SMOKING OPIUM IN MOSCOW

SMOKING OPIUM IN MOSCOW

ROGER CALDWELL

All rights reserved. No part of this work covered by the copyright herein may be reproduced or used in any means—graphic, electronic, or mechanical, including copying, recording, taping, or information storage and retrieval systems—without written permission of the publisher.

Printed by imprintdigital
Upton Pyne, Exeter
www.digital.imprint.co.uk

Typesetting by narrator
www.narrator.me.uk
info@narrator.me.uk
033 022 300 39

Published by Shoestring Press
19 Devonshire Avenue, Beeston, Nottingham, NG9 1BS
(0115) 925 1827
www.shoestringpress.co.uk

First published 2020
© Copyright: Roger Caldwell
© Cover photography by Ant Rozetsky on Unsplash

The moral right of the author has been asserted.

ISBN 978-1-912524-39-6

ACKNOWLEDGEMENTS

To: The Antigonish Review (*Canada*), The Dalhousie Review (*Canada*), Dream Catcher, French Literary Review, The Interpreter's House, Other Poetry, Pennine Platform, Philosophy Now, Poetry (*Chicago*), Poetry New Zealand.

Earlier versions of some of these poems appeared in the pamphlet collection *Walking on the Moon* (Ninth Arrondissement Press).

"There are no foreign lands.
It is the traveller only who is foreign."

– Robert Louis Stevenson, *The Silverado Squatters*

CONTENTS

(1)

Ariadne Lonely on the Shore	3
The End of Thorolf Twist-foot	5
Mount Fuji	7
Letter from Transylvania	9
The Time-Traveller's Moustache	11
A Plea for the Dead	13
On Ithaca	14
Of Gods and Men	15
The Great Highway	17

(2)

Horace Walpole on Heaven	25
Bishop Berkeley on Ideas	27
Francois Couperin at Versailles	29
The Same Difference	30
Budapest 1945: The End of the Bourgeoisie	32
A Taste of Gun-Oil	33
Blood on the Keys: The Case of Comrade Shostakovich	35
Sir Anthony Confesses	37

(3)

Tristes Tropiques	41
Nothing like St Albans	43
Going to Coventry	44
Smoking Opium in Moscow	46
The Mountains of Essex	48
A Capacity for Kindness	50
Living in Cyberspace	51
The Purpose of It All	53
Notes	56

(1)

ARIADNE LONELY ON THE SHORE

She is Ariadne, is King Minos' daughter,
stands dishevelled on the beach of Naxos,
staring out to sea

where, distant, irretrievable,
the sails and masts of Theseus' ship
dip beneath a grey horizon.

She is too numbed with grief as yet
to have ears to hear or eyes to see
what's fallen from the sky to land behind her

with conches, cymbals, horns, and shrieks
of wild-haired maenads, laughing satyrs—
the chariot of Bacchus drawn by cheetahs.

Already he's jumped down from it,
the boyish god, his velvet cloak
half-blown away from him in his excitement.

He lips are parted, eager for her mouth—
soon she will turn to meet those hungry eyes,
the moment's only half a breath away.

The sky is of a brilliant blue—
only from a sky like this
can something come that's heaven-sent—

but it's thoughts of Theseus that fill her head
who will somewhere meet his doom, she hopes,
though nothing in the picture tells us so:

here he is present only as an absence.
It's the lusty god with his exotic entourage
that makes this not an empty but a crowded scene,

one rich with promises of things to come—
that grieving Ariadne, having lost a hero,
might in a god's arms find some recompense.

THE END OF THOROLF TWIST-FOOT

(after *Eyrbyggja Saga*)

The old man was more trouble to us dead
    than when alive, although alive he'd been
trouble enough—cantankerous and mean,
    and with blood on his hands. He'd had a dispute
with Snorri the Priest over Krakaness Wood
    and when his own son refused to help
he returned to his house in a hideous rage,
    sat haughty on his high-seat, said not a word,
just sat there and glowered. We retired to bed,
    next morning found him still seated there,
features stiff, eyes set in a sullen glare,
    his body stave-straight. No doubt he'd died
of the anger within him. We were none of us sad
    to know that a tyrant's days were ended
but dragged the corpse outside, closed up its eyes,
    wrapped rags around that unloved head—
with a yoke of oxen hitched up to a sled
    drove the body up through Thorsardale
to its burial-place beneath a heaped-up cairn.
    Hard to know what we did wrong that afternoon,
except perhaps to celebrate too soon
    that the man was gone whom all detested—
even Arnkel, Thorolf's son, a man
    better by far than his father was,
though of almost anyone that could be said.
    An eagle flew across the frozen fjord
against a sudden blaze of sun, and this we took
    as portent: all was well, we thought,
but soon found that it wasn't so, instead
    this hateful man returned again, his ghost
was seen on hill-sides, then in people's houses,
    sitting by fire-sides, malevolent in death
as he had been in life, and drawing others
    to his place of doom. Because of him

all the valley was infected with disease, decay.
    There seemed no end of it. So off we went,
the bravest first, to Thorolf Twist-Foot's knoll,
    broke down the cairn, and opened up the grave,
saw a corpse no worm had dared to touch,
    intact, but swollen to a monstrous size,
more like an ox's than a man's. We tried,
    and tried again, and it took all our strength
to lift the monstrous relict out which we then rolled
    down to the foreshore where we gathered wood
in a great pyre about the body, lit a flame
    that would reduce that loathsome bulk to ashes—
once it had caught stood joyously around,
    heard with every crackling sound a step
toward deliverance from his curse
    and all the mischiefs he had caused.
A great gale now blew up, and flew his ashes out
    to distant seas, to countries far from ours,
where he may do his worst—but as for us,
    we are free from that malignant man at last.

MOUNT FUJI

There were separate pillows
    but they shared
        a single bed.

When daylight pierced
    the bamboo blinds
        they rubbed their eyes,

heard frogs croaking
    in the pond, and cries
        of wild geese flying overhead.

By now, she tells him,
    cherry-trees in Kyoto
        will be out in flower.

In the afternoon
    she lay drowsing
        in the summer garden—

blossom from a plum-tree
    fell into her open mouth,
        disturbed her dream

of snow falling on Mount Fuji—
    this she took as sign
        of happiness to come.

The seasons changed.
    Snow is deep, thick, heavy
        on Mount Fuji.

Leaves in the garden,
    frozen, crackle
        underneath her feet,

the pond's iced over,
    and a solitary crow
        perches, silent,

scarcely moving,
    on a bare unbending brittle
        plum-tree's branch.

LETTER FROM TRANSYLVANIA

The prospect from here is magnificent—
his castle's built over a precipice,
and you can see below
silvery threads where rivers wind
their ways through gorges.
There is deep forest all around.
It is a lonely somewhat eerie place.

I hear the howling of wolves by night—
their sound disturbed my dreams at first
so close it seemed to the castle walls—
but I've come to take it for granted by now,
most nights I sleep as sound as a babe.

My room is a spacious and comfortable one,
and I have use of the library
which has many strange and antique books,
most untouched, it seems, for years.
There's ample leisure to peruse them—
some recompense for lack of company.

I never see the Count by day,
he's much occupied with preparations
for transferring his effects to England.
He comes to me at night with legal questions.
I answer them as best I can—
that's why I was sent here after all—
but he seems a strange, unnatural man.

The ways of Transylvania, I find,
are not like ours. The Count,
so secluded, isolated in himself,
seems to have no need of human sympathy.
His face is bloodless. When he smiles—
it's rare enough—that smile reveals
the whiteness, sharpness of his teeth.

But this monotony takes its toll.
Truth to say I've begun to get nervous.
Wings are always flapping at my window—
bats, I presume, but why so many?
I keep a crucifix at the head of my bed,
something I've never done before,
but it makes me feel safe, although by day
I'm tempted to laugh at my foolishness.

It's not that anything is amiss,
but I want to shrug off this solitude.
I shall be glad when our business is done
and I can say goodbye to the Count's affairs.
There's something of death about this place—
I've had my fill of howling wolves,
of enigmas, of wild forsaken places.
and long to be released, to be returned
to friends I miss, to the woman I love,
to see the sunrise over Hampstead Hill.

THE TIME-TRAVELLER'S MOUSTACHE

He carried with him a small valise
though we never saw him open it.
His appearance was unremarkable—

even his moustache was commonplace.
He seemed to have no family, no friends,
but exuded a sense of loneliness.

We caught the trace of a London accent,
but the way that he spoke, so slow, precise,
as if he pondered every word

before he said it made one think
he was translating from a foreign language.
We found him comical almost—

elaborate manners and antique attire
set him apart from the rest of the human race.
He was of another time than ours—

He could knock back pints like the best of the lads,
but had no place in a London pub.
He was always fingering his moustache

as if he found it a kind of burden.
Why have one at all if that was the case?
Or was it a part of his disguise?

As the evening rolled on we joked and laughed,
and he played his part in the merriment
in his own way—eyes darting everywhere,

and finding marvels in all they saw—
pool-table, dartboard, shabby décor—
in all that to us was nondescript.

Not that he said so—or not to us.
For all his apparent bonhomie
he was no less a walking enigma.

In the end curiosity proved too much.
We traipsed upstairs to his hotel room,
knocked on the door, then pushed it open—

only to find we had come too late.
It was as if he had never been there.
He had departed abruptly from the scene,

left nothing behind, no trace of his presence—
except, as we saw, round the rim of the basin
where he had shaved—an abundance of hairs.

Whatever the time or place he'd gone to
he had chosen to leave—no doubt for good reasons—
with his valise, but without his moustache.

A PLEA FOR THE DEAD

No one wants to know you when you're dead
though they liked you well enough, it seemed,
when you could just about hang on,

with *You're looking well* and *You'll pull through*
or *We'll see you down the pub next week.*
It's different once you've kicked the bucket—

they avert their eyes, won't mention your name:
it's as if you were guilty of some crime
so obscene no one dares mention it.

True, you don't look at your best when dead,
you're not skin and bone any more, just bone—
and the grin of a skull has an ugly look.

This can't be helped—but it's not to the point.
There's nothing shameful in having died,
nor to be proud of in staying alive.

They say we've passed on to a better place,
but we've not gone away—we can't, we're dead.
Yet we're rather a large minority group,

and if it's wrong to discriminate
on grounds of gender or colour or class,
isn't it time to honour those deceased,

to allow them their dignity, their rights,
not to turn the cold shoulder—as you all do—
to shoulders so much colder still?

ON ITHACA

True, you have something of the looks he had
if reports are right,
but so much could be said of many.

Even if you are the one you say you are
that doesn't mean—since times have changed—
that you are any less a stranger.

Not only Ithaca, the world itself
is now another place
than any you might still lay claim to.

Old mariner, you've travelled far—
time makes of all of us a foreigner
to what we thought was ours.

Young heroes set out many years ago
to Troy aboard their long-oared ships.
There were, I think, reports of war.

But memories are short.
There comes a point of no return.
In Ithaca we have new concerns

that have no bearing on our old mishaps.
You have an antique way of speech.
It has no meaning to us now.

OF GODS AND MEN

Immortals, dwellers on Olympus heights,
pursue their abstruse pleasures—
no reason they should pay regard
to toilers in the valley far below.

There humans are preoccupied
with drawing bare subsistence from a stony soil,
don't look up much to the mist and clouds
encircling the mountain-top,
and if they think of deities
they're other deities than those that are.

What, though, if curiosity,
or bliss in surfeit, led a god
down to the valley and the world of men?
It's a moot point what good he'd find there—
whether gods should also learn
what mere humans have to teach.

His godliness would seem plain awkward,
be cause for laughter if he hadn't wings
to raise him to the heights again.
Work of humans he'd find hard,
rough to his unpractised hands.

What would he find if he returned?
Would he still have a place among Olympians,
his tongue, once honeyed, stained
with men's words, their heresies,
his divinity in tatters now?

Oracles fell silent, men
doubted of the gods
who'd doubted first of them,
and up the mountain-side
there's such cloud you'll never find a path that's true,
or track of anyone to know
if they aspired, or fell.

                      As for myself:
you'll find me of an afternoon
drowsing—when I'm able—in an easy-chair
far from Olympus and the valley now,
resolved to climb no farther up
for fear of falling further down,
not answering to gods or men,
unwilling to be judged by either.

THE GREAT HIGHWAY

We soon lost count. An hour passed,
and still more soldiers' feet tramped by—
armed warriors with shields and spears

raised dust along the great highway.
Wagons followed, laden with provisions—
they creaked with women, food, and wine.

After them, in costly clothes, on palfreys
rode physicians, alchemists, astrologers,
on foot a fool, and seven dwarves with boxes.

On hushed wheels, at a respectful distance,
the gilded carriage of the emperor arrived,
vast, slow, so bright it hurt one's eyes to look—

we weren't allowed to see his face, of course.
Lackeys in livery with pomaded hair
rode by on ponies, waving handkerchiefs—

their perfume hung suspended in the dust-filled air—
and on high horses the imperial guard
with scimitars and harsh disdainful faces.

There were others of the royal entourage—
master of the chessboard, of the imperial privy,
priests with beards and talismans,

and, it was whispered, half his harem
who travelled in rich, and curtained, coaches.
(His catamites had their own pavilion.)

Half-naked men led lynxes past on leashes.
Chattering monkeys, squeaking pigs were managed—
or almost so—by boys with sticks.

We were children then and easily impressed—
Of all the wonders that we saw that day
it was elephants that amazed us most—

we'd not known there were such beasts on earth.
But the show was almost over, soon the last cadets
with drums and flutes had passed us by,

barefoot stragglers too had disappeared
with all the long procession up into the mountains.
Dust and silence fell along the great highway.

We stood there at the roadside as night fell
as if we had awoken from a dream
too soon, and couldn't face reality.

In succeeding days, months, years
we saw nothing we might wonder at,
only pedlars, beggars, solitary quacks,

herdsmen with bedraggled cows.
There was a dearth of travellers with news
to tell of victories or defeats.

Yet in that dearth strange rumours came,
though where they came from no one knew—
that the emperor's army had been all for show,

never faced an enemy, nor was intended to,
its only end to awe the populace
so they'd remain compliant to imperial rule.

Others said there was no emperor at all,
he, his army, entourage a poet's fictions,
or that the great highway itself was nothing great,

a mere unfinished country road, and leading nowhere.
We who lived beside it couldn't credit this,
nor believe that what we'd seen had been a counterfeit,

though, having lived drab lives and in drab times so long,
with nothing marvellous to see or do
for all our waiting, watching, through decades,

we came to wonder what it was we'd seen,
and if as adults we could see what children saw.
Miracles had vanished from our world, it seemed.

But then one day a distant cloud of dust
out from the mountains spread across the plain
and down along the great highway—

we heard, though faint, a sound of tramping feet,
thronged to the roadside, hope was in our eyes
to see the long procession come. It came—

but much changed, diminished in the interim
from what it once had been. Not over-mighty now,
and whether battle-scarred or merely scarred by time,

old soldiers who'd once marched came limping by
on emaciated limbs, their eyes averted,
and no pennants flying. They all looked half-starved,

more ghosts of themselves than living men.
Few carriages, but jolting wagons—carts
bore unruly, drunken, and blaspheming women,

surely such as never graced a royal harem.
The imperial coach, no longer golden now,
was like some spoilt child's discarded toy—

axles creaked as it came lumbering by,
one door swung open on a broken hinge.
Hard to tell if someone lurked inside.

A sullen jester, still with cap and bells,
mouthed curses underneath his breath.
Drummer boys could scarcely beat their drums.

A tall gaunt man, black mask across his face,
in silent fury waved a rusted axe—
like an executioner whose victim had escaped.

Of all the elephants a single one was left
and that so shrivelled, feeble, woebegone,
unfit to bear a catafalque

we would have laughed had we not pitied him.
A handful of retainers, wheeling barrows, showed
a box of unexploded fireworks,

a pair of antiquated clocks as salvage,
a jumble of assorted bric-à-brac.
Two cowled monks with begging-bowls,

small frightened children with bewildered eyes
who tried to sell us withered flowers in baskets
brought the sorry circus to an end—

only monkeys, mischievous, and scampering about,
brought life, youth, energy, and merriment
as if they mocked the moribund parade,

itself grotesque, with more grotesqueries.
Some scrambled up into our arms, pulled at our hair,
chattered nonsense in our ears as we stood there,

last watchers by the great highway.
When all else had disappeared
they stayed with us—are with us still,

seem almost human with their senseless talk,
their wizened faces too much like our own.
We've no need of vigils. In these afterdays

we tilled our fields, resumed our former ways,
sat at evening by the hearth and drank mulled wine,
jostled children's children on arthritic knees.

We don't choose to fill their ears with what we've seen—
since nothing new will come along the great highway
that's not another sort of nothingness.

(2)

HORACE WALPOLE ON HEAVEN

It's time to be done with worldly matters—
with the aid of laudanum and asafoetida
I'll part with this pretty vision, life.
I must send a letter to Lady Hervey
to thank her for the potted pilchards—
and to inform her I shall need no more.

Habitué of gloomy nooks and arches,
enthusiast for Etruscan vases—
it was my fate to be a dilettante.
When my gilder laid on the last leaf of gold
I knew my homeland was Strawberry Hill.

I'll find it no hardship not having to dine
at Lord Archer's again (such an odious man),
Mrs Fitzroy in a Turkish dress
won't detain me now, and I shan't shed tears
if no invitation from Hatfield comes.

Such an idle journey I have made of things,
I'm the hero only of my nothingness,
so *isolé,* so far withdrawn, so set apart
from anything that matters in the world
that when my little lamp goes out
it will be scarcely missed—
even I myself will scarcely miss it.

So: a sprig of rosemary, if you must,
but no laurels, please. I had never thought
I needed to be born, but when I found I was—
well, then I was forced to improvise.
My castle with its gingerbread glories
wasn't built to last,
like me was only of its time.

I lived as life's obscurest passenger,
a virtuoso of irrelevance—and as for love,
it never once scaled my battlements.
I can only hope it's not heretical
to think there may be laughter in the world to come,
and quaintness, oddity, and to hope that heaven
is a place that resembles Strawberry Hill.

BISHOP BERKELEY ON IDEAS

They laugh at me, they say I eat and drink Ideas,
that I have banished from the world
all that's solid, have made dreams, chimeras
out of everything that men hold certain—
they say I am mad, but you know I am not,
my dear: you are as real to me as I to you,
and as are both of us to God.

So too with kitchen, garden, parlour chairs.
Yet if our wise Creator
for one moment turned His gaze away
(He won't, of course) then this abundant fabric
would vanish utterly, our world be gone—
all would perish in an instant.

The common man knows better than philosophers
that if all our senses were closed off
there would be nothing to be seen or known,
that mere clods of earth lack all reality
without a mind in which they have existence.
How could leaves rustle, grass be green
if no spirit had conceived, and then perceived, them?

If this is madness then most men are mad.
John Locke himself admits
he can't say wherein its essence lies,
this substance he so much insists upon
that he calls matter—but a stone
is no less a stone when it exists as an Idea.

Green fields yonder, and the sun that shines
above us—this rich world of ours
is no mere dream, I never said it was.
Why must they misconceive me so?

Your hand in my hand, dear, is real enough,
and gives real warmth, and there is life and love,
all in the perspective of God's eye—
and a surplusage immeasurable of things.

FRANCOIS COUPERIN AT VERSAILLES

The rooms seemed infinite; the mirrors
mirrored infinities beyond
of gilded emptiness. Upstairs
a monkey scampered, parrot screeched,
spoilt children laughed. Outside were lawns,
were statues, fountains; paths
led out towards the vanishing-point.

In a wilderness of damasks and brocades
servants fawned and courtiers conspired.
Polite, the little clavicinist played
to a periwig and red-heeled slippers
badineries until the guests dispersed.

Afterwards, in evening's cool,
His Majesty with last late guests
strolled past illuminated lakes
where fountains threw up jets of water
in intricate designs of coloured lights.

Within, the little clavecinist played,
alone, impromptus, hidden thoughts
en blanc et noir. The sounds
were lost down miles of frigid corridors
where no one listened as his music caught,
past persiflage and jeux d'amour,
a plodding rhythm, joined the onward march
out from the campagne, of bitter men
across the distant fields, across decades
to Paris, and the rumbling wheels
of laborious carts to tumbrels
over cobbled streets.

THE SAME DIFFERENCE

It need never have happened—
had there been good harvests
and the king proved stronger-willed,
if the Bastille had never fallen
or the Duchesse d'Orléans' coach
not been admitted through the barricades,
there would have been no Revolution,
no cataclysm come to shake the world.
It could so easily have been different.

It's the same with you and I, my friend.
We're likewise accidents of fate.
Had our parents never met that night,
or had they met a moment later
the spermatozoon and the egg
would have brought into the world another child—
the merest impulse changes history,
creates new happiness, new misery.
It could so easily have been different.

Or else perhaps the scene was set:
it required no Marie Antoinette.
After decades of mismanagement,
a nobility hardened against change
(for reasons that themselves had roots)
the merest detail was enough
this year or the next to lay the charge,
a single spark to set the whole thing off.
It would all have happened anyway.

It's the same with you and I, my love.
Whatever we might do or say
forces within us, and without,
were not to be of our own making
but were laid down in the distant past.
Lettres de cachet had already failed:
a word broke down the Bastille door.
No word could raise it up again.
It would all have happened anyway.

BUDAPEST 1945: THE END OF THE BOURGEOISIE

"The cross he carried was to be a bourgeois."
— Sándor Márai

It's no time for health-cures, laxatives,
or expensive hair-oils bought from London—
hang up your antiquated double-breasted suit,
pinstripes will be out for a good while yet.
No one blows his nose into silk handkerchiefs—
or what are fingers for?

Time's past for writing polished letters
to editors of literary magazines
now hero-plumbers rule the scene,
now *altmodisch* countesses abase themselves
at roadside stalls by selling doughnuts,
though still acting supercilious—
as if to sniff the common air
were to take poison.

Germans leave, the Russians come.
Houses of the rich are ruined, plundered
in a city where all bridges are demolished
so you cannot cross from Buda into Pest.
At once-exclusive restaurants all may dine—
if only on a meal of caterpillar soup.

They prick up their ears and purse their lips,
remember concerts at the Gellert Hall,
as if their glory days might come again,
as if bourgeois culture weren't beyond recall—

as if in days to come
someone might listen to a string quartet,
or pare his nails, or simply read a book.

A TASTE OF GUN-OIL

El Floridita—at the corner of the bar
he watched Constantino mix daiquiris,

a bar-room brawler, one might think,
but it's the old man and the sea again—

outriggers have been baited, set,
teasers are zigzagging in blue water,

then the marlin hits. That old whore death,
no need to seek her, never far away.

Spain has its oxcarts still, and gypsy women
cooking stews at the horsefair—

Basque girls dance, and maddened bulls
charge over cobblestones, and boys

brave horns again at the *encierro*
as in the glory days. But as for now

truth is in the mirror, grey hair combed
forward to disguise a balding head,

is testosterone drugs, a swollen liver,
sleeplessness, and paranoia.

No liquor—"It's as if you'd drive a racing-car
but have no oil for lubrication."

It would maybe have been better
if he'd not seen her in the Venice rain—

the muse has left no forwarding address.
A taste of gun-oil fills his mouth.

Batista and his friends have fled,
Castro's rebels down from the hills,

informers found dead with their tongues cut out.
La Finca Vigía has twenty-two cats.

The dangerous summer comes to Rochester.
Electrodes to his head. In a locked wing

of the Mayo Clinic all-night lights are burning..
In La Finca's garden with its reds and blues

jacaranda blossoms float in pools,
air's sweet with scent of frangipani.

In Idaho two twelve-gauge shells explode.
The bedside-table clock ticks on, on, on.

BLOOD ON THE KEYS: THE CASE OF COMRADE SHOSTAKOVICH

A nervous pale bespectacled young man
  who plays in movie-houses for his bread.
    Is deficient in Marxist-Leninist theory.

He peers at the world through heavy lenses.
  He bites his nails, they're stained with nicotine.
    His music—what we've heard of it—

seems rather vehement. He played for us
  his piano sonata. Once he'd left
    we saw that there was blood on the keys.

They don't doubt his talent, only find it hard to see
  how socialism will be better for it.
    But he'll acquire a grasp of dialectics,

in the interests of a greater cause he'll scorn
  reactionary formalist aesthetics,
    bourgeois individualistic traits,

will find social meaning in the timbral aggregates
  of Alexander Scriabin, and—very late—
    will even condescend to join the Party.

True, there'll be problems—in hard times to come,
  once Bukharin has been tried and shot, and Meyerhold
    and Mandelstam have left the scene,

he will spend nights sitting up, his suitcase packed,
  wait for the knock at the door that means
    it's time to join his confrères in the Gulag.

In the Khruschev thaw—still traumatized—he'll write,
    to nondescript obsequious verses,
        a paean to afforestation,

will be the public man with thin-lipped smile
    who visits schools, collective farms
        and factories—he'll even sign,

his head bent down, the letter against Sakharov,
    lament his drab and miserable life,
        all the official lies, will die

high summer, 1975. His funeral,
    one worthy of a major "Soviet artist",
        will take place at an unlucky time

when orchestras are out of town,
    so when Chopin's Funeral March strikes up
        it will be butchered by a military band,

and over his grave there will be speeches,
    stale, lengthy, platitudinous,
        by Khrennikov and other stalwarts

of the Ministry of Culture—not a note
    of his own music will be heard
        on that unseasonably chilly afternoon.

SIR ANTHONY CONFESSES

"Working for Stalin? No, not so…
When Whittaker Chambers met his 'ghost'
from the Comintern he had no thought
of betraying his country.
It was only to aid the better side—
the world was divided, Fascists and Reds,
and nothing of substance in between."

They tire of his patrician drawl,
they're of another time and class than his,
find his ways exquisite. They have questions
he can't brush off with an eloquent sleeve.

"Do you know your history, my friends?
Torchlight parades, the tramp of boots
of arrest squads down the Friedrichstrasse,
a new political internment camp
in a modest little German town…
Show trials in Moscow had begun.
Hollywood starlets funded the cause,
they all had friends in the Politburo.
They—we— were naïve, but nobody thought
the Red Flag would fly from Buckingham Palace
or commissars come to Tammany Hall.
The promised land was not without its faults,
but when the war was won it was due in part
to the man the press called Uncle Joe."

He falters, can't find the words he wants,
gestures to paintings on the walls:
"Art and politics are not the same, of course.
The greatest of painters makes mistakes,
leaves smudges on the canvas. But in politics
such smudges may bring death to millions.
It was another era. Such barbarities—"

They cut him short. There's silence in the room.
He senses they resent his old-world manners,
that they care little for his paintings.
He turns his back on his inquisitors,
looks out the window into Portman Square—
the view is at its best in spring-time—
then turns again to face them,
drains his glass, and says:

"Yes, gentlemen, it's true, I was a spy for Stalin.
Do with me what you think it's best to do."

(3)

TRISTES TROPIQUES
i.m. Claude Lévi-Strauss (1908–2009)

He hates all travellers, and travellers' tales—
the mind itself is an exotic place,
and it is as if
he never ventured far beyond the parquet floor,
Paris seemed so much his natural habitat.

But colonialist lies and missionaries' myths
once drew him out into the tropics, where he trod
the red soil of Brazil
in baggy shorts, crossed boggy tracks,
pith-helmeted and seeking *indigènes*.

In southlands, squinting through binoculars,
he sees at last, camped by the river-side,
naked, somnolent,
feet trailing in the muddy water, men,
though of another kind than his—Bororos—

unconscious bricoleurs of symbols, signs,
unaware of any need to be "discovered"
or "interpreted",
but themselves sufficient to themselves,
who'd thought their world the only world that was.

Newcomer to ramshackle villages,
to smouldering camp-fires, semi-feral dogs,
he is to them
a new species of exotica, though one, it seems,
strangely ignorant of the laws of kinship.

They couldn't know—they had no need to know—
their cosmos was only one of many,
that their way of life
was now a list of words, reduced to structures,
put into a book, made obsolete.

Je haïs les voyages et les voyageurs.
A centenarian, his veiny hands reach out,
bespeckled, slow,
to hold firm to the twisting rail that leads
up to the mezzanine of the *laboratoire*

d'anthropologie sociale—his intellectual home—
sad tropics long behind him. Each day, it seems,
the distance grows
between his office and the turbid muddy flow
of a Brazilian river, Nambikwara girls

giggling in rock-pools, and he is now
almost museum of himself, sole member
of a tribe
that's otherwise extinct, exotic remnant
of a species that's all totem and taboo

to modern eyes. The girl-reporter asks:
"What of your works do you think will survive?"
He can only reply
to one of another time, another world than his:
"As for all that, I neither know nor care."

NOTHING LIKE ST ALBANS

A quiet tree-lined avenue,
those who lived there solid respectable folk—
the sort who went to church on Sundays.

All in all a decorous decent place—
cars didn't hoot, or children shout.
Even dogs were well-behaved.

When you looked out of a landing window
there was nothing to see but houses and trees
and your own little patch of Hertfordshire sky.

No one was rich but no one was poor.
Hedges were trimmed, and lawns well-mown.
There was no reason for things to change.

School reinforced a neighbourly ethics—
Mediocria firma was its motto
translated as "firm middle way".

When he left—at last—for the world outside
it was to find he had been ill-prepared
for what lurks at the end of an avenue

and is alien to an English market town.
He was first appalled, and then relieved, to find
the world was nothing like St Albans

GOING TO COVENTRY

The window-pane keeps misting up
so close he presses his face against it.
He has been waiting there forever,
but now at last he sees it glide
around the corner, come to a halt
in front of his house—
the Humber Super Snipe.

The driver's Uncle Eric, there beside him
Auntie Ruth, and in the dark interior
a wizened old lady with a budgerigar
who, as he knows, is Uncle Eric's mother.
He and his parents will complete the party.
The Humber Super Snipe has room for all.

They are going to Coventry, they say,
to see the cathedral, but to him
the Humber's cathedral in itself,
there's so much of it to marvel at—
tassels to cling to, occasional seats,
chair-backs that magically open up
to serve as tables, and everywhere
shine, feel, pungent tang of leather.

It purrs on its way like a nonchalant cat,
noses on to empty motorways
out from forgotten 1950s streets.

Coventry bores him, he thought it would.
The party's subdued on its long way back,
he doesn't know why
He's perched on the lap of Auntie Ruth,
immersed in her gift of *Treasure Island*—
his fingers make tears in the flimsy pages
as he fumbles to know what will happen next.

He's long since reached the end of the book—
it's many years later he discovers
that he was present in another story
where what matters is what doesn't happen,
where Uncle Eric won't marry Auntie Ruth
(the dried-up old lady will see to that,
and will only die when they've broken things off),
and he'd been the child they would never have.

Of the six in the Humber he's sole survivor,
no longer a trusting freckle-faced kid,
but set in his ways into sterner stuff.
Eric and Ruth left the world before their time,
old age took others in due course—
his mother, impossibly old and deaf,
gave up the ghost a half a century after—
and the Humber, even then an antique,
was doubtless long ago sold for scrap.

He has read *Treasure Island* through and through,
has never gone back to Coventry since.

SMOKING OPIUM IN MOSCOW

The young Iranian apologized—
"My brother back in Teheran's an addict,
I've been smoking with him every day.
I must have a little just to help me sleep."

I joined him, as no doubt he'd hoped I would.
He prepared a cigarette with practised hands,
and then another—as we smoked
there came a sense of calm and peace,
all sense of time slowed down.
In the end we sat up through the night,
saw a greyish Moscow dawn rise up,
watched from our hotel window
early morning workers cross the square below,
toy-like figures to our eyes.

We snatched an hour of sleep at most,
his no doubt as dream-filled as was mine,
before the summons came for us to leave
if we were to catch the flight to London.

Our seats were far apart, my opium-friend
I never saw again—and as the plane took off,
left Soviet ground, and soared into the clouds—
my head itself was cloud-like too,
I was neither quite awake nor quite asleep
but drifting in a sort of inner space.

When Aeroflot's hot meals arrived
I played vacantly with plastic knife and fork
just enough to snatch up some small scraps,
left my dish of Russian caviare untouched,
was somewhere else and in another time
when the plane nosed down and with a jolt
hit Heathrow, England, and normality.

That evening, after many months away,
I made for the pub to meet old friends—
reassuring mugs of English beer
stood on tables, only I had changed.
It had been a long way back to Hertfordshire,
only part of me had yet arrived,
the rest was in another country.

I listened in, absorbed the local news—
how Melanie had taken up with Tim,
why no one went to the Wheatsheaf any more.
I told them, when they asked, about Iran,
but only what I thought they'd like to hear.
I never said that on the night before
I'd been in Moscow smoking opium—
it was nothing, after all, of world-significance,
only to myself did it make sense—
but that I felt the need to hold my tongue,
to listen to their stories, not tell mine,
made for a difference, opened up
a gap between us that could not be closed.

THE MOUNTAINS OF ESSEX

For Rousseau no flat country could suffice,
only landscapes were sublime
that could provoke a sense of terror,
that showed mankind its insignificance
against the might of nature, and for this
mountains, precipices, torrents were required—
of which, of course, there are none in Essex.

He would have scorned its slowly-flowing rivers,
marshes, muddy fields of placid sheep,
quaint villages. He would have said:
There's nothing that's sublime in Essex.

To prove him wrong would be an uphill task,
and here there are no hills to climb,
but merely flatlands.
                            Things are changed today:
overnight much snow has fallen
and made familiar pathways vanish,
changed green fields to wintry wastes—
there's a loss of boundaries, of long perspectives,
and wide Essex skies—occluded—
threaten there's more snow to come.

The scene outside my window is a challenge:
I turn TV and central heating off,
brave myself for confronting what's sublime
(or almost so). Relieved from human pettiness,
I arm myself against outrageous weather
with hat, thick gloves, thick overcoat,
my feet encased in Russian fur-lined boots,
sturdy for scaling fells or mountain-sides—
of which, as we know, there are none in Essex.

I set out into another country now,
trudge across these vanished fields,
all the world about me whitened
to a blank expanse of wilderness
as I recede into the distance,
dwindle to less than a dot in the eye,
on my way toward sublimity
via the vanishing-point.

A CAPACITY FOR KINDNESS

I should have lied: a defiant *No*
would have served both better than a guilty *Yes*
to the question that she asked that day.

Confessions should be heard by priests
in secret—not be blurted out
to those who might be hurt by them.

Truth's a matter for philosophers,
but for the rest of us
too much of it brings loneliness.

It's simpler in the end to deal in fictions.
Now I know what's best to say when love comes in—
it's to my shame I didn't know it then—

for truth's of no importance in our lives:
what matters most
is a capacity for kindness, and for telling lies.

LIVING IN CYBERSPACE

Here you pay for your passage with virtual money
but Musical Chairs is played for real,
though rules of the game are changed mid-play
so you never end up where you thought you were
    but find you occupy a space

that bears the sign: Reserved for Others.
Even expiry dates are not what they seem,
more reminders of the provisional basis
on which you exist, so up-grades come
    always without a guarantee

that convenience shopping is yours forever.
Your name is a label on the clothes you wear,
identity's changed with a change of shoes,
and ecological footprints are to be counted
    on a sliding scale

as trauma becomes a way of life
now slimming down, and phasing out,
and loss of collective bargaining power
mean you're on your own unless you can snatch
    a new way of being

from an analyst's couch or a motel bed.
In post-industrialist wastelands you must learn
how to make a theme-park by yourself
with items bought on-line, recycled from
    remaindered life-style magazines.

We are ourselves collections of spare parts
much subject to the laws of obsolescence—
none of the instructions we were given
tell us what re-assembly of them
    could make a living working whole.

We've strayed beyond our credit limit,
only shopping-malls are built to last,
Health-clubs make you fit not healthy
but no one will say what you'll be fit for
    unless it is to undergo

your trainer's next regime—since even death
will come with a repayment package,
postponed until, no longer user-friendly,
your password gives you entry to a text
    that, once unscrambled,

greets you with the message: File Deleted.
We are hardware running software programmes,
are our own encryptions of ourselves.
We'd not recognize each other if we met.
    I am not I, you are not you,

all we exchanged was someone else's e-mails
at the Café Med in Colchester
or in Braintree's New York Deli.
Who do our ring-tones answer to
    now that we live in cyberspace?

THE PURPOSE OF IT ALL

First it was required
that there be four fundamental forces—
electromagnetic, gravitational,
weak, and strong—
and these refined to an improbable degree
so that atoms may be formed, and stars,
exploding supernovae from whose dust
and after many billion years
a planet might revolve around a middling sun,
and on that planet blobs of DNA.

It was necessary, then,
that there be protozoa, metazoa
and arthropods invading land,
Cretaceous flowers,
the dinosaurs (and their demise),
monotremes, marsupials, and man.
Then after mitochondrial Eve
had found her brood in Adam
there must come history, religion, war,
the invention of the wheel,
and Aristotle's metaphysics,
Lindbergh crossing the Atlantic,
telegraphy, and William Butler Yeats—
and me.

All this was needed:
a universe so many light-years wide,
a multitude of creatures who,
once born, must die,
catastrophe, apocalypse,
a false messiah and (perhaps) a true,
and all to this effect—

that I, Roger Caldwell,
having had a drink at the Rose and Crown,
the pub on the quayside,
should stumble home across the field
on a humid Wednesday evening
early in a new millennium,
sit at my desk and there scrawl out,
for reasons no one could predict,
a poem that would then explain
"the purpose of it all".

Yes.

And now the poem's written.

NOTES

Ariadne Lonely on the Shore: This is an interpretation of Titian's painting of Bacchus and Ariadne, currently in London's National Gallery. I have seen it many times without quite understanding it.

A Plea for the Dead: Here I have invented a new form of political correctness.

The Great Highway: The narrator, it scarcely needs to be said, is an unreliable one, though there is no reason to suppose that he shares the casual misogyny of the world he describes.

Bishop Berkeley on Ideas: This is, inter alia, a corrective to Yeats' famous account of Berkeley as presenting us with a dream-world that would perish "if the mind but change its theme". For Berkeley reality was guaranteed by the perception of God whose mind would never "change its theme".

A Taste of Gun-Oil: The world has no great need of a poem on the death (by suicide) of Ernest Hemingway. Nonetheless I have supplied one, seeing him as the victim of his own machismo.

Sir Anthony Confesses: This is, of course, Sir Anthony Blunt, art historian, erstwhile Surveyor of the Queen's Pictures, and spy for Stalin. His apology here is not as consequential as it might have been.

Tristes Tropiques: In the 1970s Claude Lévi-Strauss was a fashionable guru whose works drew many (myelf included) to the study of social anthropology. He is nowadays by comparison little-read.

Smoking Opium in Moscow: This was in 1978, and the result of taking an Aeroflot flight from Teheran which involved an overnight stop in Moscow. When I returned to Teheran in the autumn opium-dreams would be lost to political reality with the signs of imminent revolution.

Living in Cyberspace: The metaphor of Musical Chairs being played for real comes from the late Zygmunt Bauman (1925–2017), the sociologist of "liquid modernity".